Out of Order

poems by

Eileen Ivey Sirota

Finishing Line Press
Georgetown, Kentucky

Out of Order

Copyright © 2019 by Eileen Ivey Sirota
ISBN 978-1-64662-307-5 First Edition
All rights reserved under International and Pan-American Copyright Conventions. No part of this book may be reproduced in any manner whatsoever without written permission from the publisher, except in the case of brief quotations embodied in critical articles and reviews.

ACKNOWLEDGMENTS

Night Court and Fiftieth Anniversary, August 28, 2013 were published in *Beltway Poetry Quarterly* Volume 19:2, 2019.
Spring Haikus were published in *District Lines* Vol. V, 2018.
Way Too Much and Not Enough and Waiting were published by *Calyx* in 2016 and 2017, respectively.
Cheney Takes a Holiday was published in *NewVerseNews* on 9/25/11.

Publisher: Leah Maines
Editor: Christen Kincaid
Cover Art: Eileen Ivey Sirota
Author Photo: 1250 Productions
Cover Design: Elizabeth Maines McCleavy

Order online: www.finishinglinepress.com
also available on amazon.com

Author inquiries and mail orders:
Finishing Line Press
P. O. Box 1626
Georgetown, Kentucky 40324
U. S. A.

Table of Contents

I.

Sneezes and Whispers 1
Fiftieth Anniversary, August 28, 2013 2
Spring Haikus 3
For D'Ane 4
The Last Speaker 5
Waiting 6
Bubbe 7
Winter Quartet 8

II.

Cheney Takes a Holiday 11
Undoing: Inauguration Day 2009 12
Apologetically White 13
Night Court 14
Gender Studies 15
Election 2016 16
How I Learned to Love the Hat 17
On the Costa Brava 18

III.

Life Out of Order 21
Way Too Much and Not Enough 22
In Praise of Praise 23
Unfinished 24
Flight Path 25
Ode to Memory Loss 26
Poor Narcissus 27
At the Registry of Regret and Injustice 28
Larger Cages, More Desire 29
Scenes from an April Evening, 1933 30

I.

Sneezes and Whispers

A visitation, you called it,
delighted when comic, thunderous sneezes
began to erupt from you,
your late father's signature sound.

Next came gouty stabs,
cardiac stuttering, sciatic whispers—
a less gentle patrimony.
Biology, you wondered? Or his displeasure?

The chiding of a humble man
for your pride
in unearned good health,
a rooster taking credit for the dawn.

Fiftieth Anniversary, August 28, 2013
(March on Washington for Jobs and Freedom, August 28, 1963)

There's something you should know about Jack:
he never ventured outside. Sun and heat
were his sworn enemies;
his deity was rest.

"Only mad dogs and Englishmen
go out in the noonday sun" was his favorite saying.
Next favorite: "never sit when you can lie down;
never stand when you can sit."

Yet there stood my father in 1963,
sweating but determined,
surrounded by thousands in jackets and ties
who would no longer lie down.

As a child he wept for the Scottsboro boys
like I now weep for Trayvon Martin. Today,
wearing this fifty-year-old button, I tend the fire
that he lit in me, on that distant August day.

Spring Haikus

in Farragut Square
shirtless Feds playing frisbee
beneath swelling buds.

    ***

a swarm of selfies
beneath a pink canopy
tourists dodge traffic.

    ***

cherry tree blossoms—
non-partisan give-away
inside the Beltway.

    ***

hollow trunk sprouts blooms
life and death dance cheek to cheek:
cherry tree lessons.

For D'Ane

Pasta and pomegranates
spices of the Orient
tomatoes to thrill the tongue and soul
a tapestry I would weave for you

steal fire from the gods
to warm you
kindle you
in your Baltimore bed

With Scheherazade's audacity
I fancied keeping you alive,
a citizen of the world, at least by proxy,
another day, week, month.

You did not wait.

The Last Speaker
(To the last speakers of the nearly 7,000 endangered languages)

The mother tongue gone,
Crept off with your last heartbeat.
With whom can I speak?

Waiting

In the anteroom, the ladies rehearse their craft.

Peaceful practices her mindful meditation,
nods off, a smile playing around her lips.

Senseless finishes a row of knitting, rips the stitches out, stands, sits,
goes to her purse to look for something, forgets what.

Unexpected bursts in like a whirlwind, a torrent of unruly hair,
still wearing yesterday's sweatpants, lists spilling urgently from her pockets.

Prolonged annoys the others. Her stories,
circles of suffering, never vary, never end.

They wait, the envoys of death, for us.

Bubbe

At dawn, you will remember
the feel of her new stockings
so cool and smooth over the bumpy tracks in her legs
(a treasure map of the Old Country, you thought),

cinnamon rolls and hot chocolate tea parties
on an age-worn cloth beneath her lilacs,
how she gave you $1.44 (real money in those days)
for a plastic tiara,
how she brushed away your mother's protest:
"It's not the whole money."

As you sit now before her coffin,
your throat like an emery board,
she has burrowed into your blood and belly,
and murmurs *shana madela, my pretty girl.*

Winter Quartet

First Snow

Season's first snowfall
Soaring sled flight, joyous squeals—
Godliness enough.

Second Snow

Outside my window
Oaks bow with courtly manners:
Winter gravitas.

Third Snow

Snow's unforeseen gift:
Silken silent symphony,
Time decelerates.

Fourth Snow

Drifts rise, tempers flare,
Swelling stacks of dirty cocoa cups—
No let-up in sight.

II.

Cheney Takes a Holiday

Cheney writes that after heart surgery in 2010, he was unconscious for weeks. During that time, the New York Times writes, Cheney had a "prolonged, vivid dream that he was living in an Italian villa, pacing the stone paths to get coffee and newspapers."

Even unconscious, Dick Cheney paces,
restless, seeking coffee
and newspapers, in an Italian villa.

Did the fennel fronds along the path
bow and quiver at his footstep,
while Tuscan winds
whispered of waterboarding?

Did the latte sour in its pot,
deposit lumps of curd
at news of his approach,
weep into the *fazzoletti*?

And what about the newspapers
with their operatic names—
Corriere della Sera,
Il Messaggero?
Did ink spill off the page
to escape his touch?

Perhaps the stones he trod
broadcast their shivers to those other
stones, standing silent, sober
in Anbar, Helmand, Alabama.

Cheney's fantasy;
Italy's *sogno brutto*.
Tell the unconscious Americans
to stay home.

Undoing: Inauguration Day 2009

At midnight we stand united in our dreaming

as if our sixty-three million pairs of hands could untie ropes,
lift down the trembling but unharmed bodies
from four thousand trees,

Blessed art Thou, Source of Light,
Spirit of the world,

as if the whips could recoil from smooth brown backs,
refurl themselves into innocent helixes,

Who has given us life,

as if babies could fly back to their mothers' arms
across half a nation and four hundred years,

as if four little girls could not go to church that day,

Sustained us,

as if the twelve million could be gathered up, ships sail eastward
across the Atlantic,
return them home strong and unbroken,

And allowed us to reach this day.

In this generous moment
we dream we can begin again,
wash ourselves clean in tears.

Apologetically White

stretched across his hard chest
two words
punch like fists:
Unapologetically black

why do I tremble?

just this morning,
every morning, I woke
in my EZ Pass white skin,

rode my fast,
unencumbered lane
of this American life

me: wanting to rinse off
the persistent stink of our history,
return to 2008, cherish my inaugural
tears of joy and self-congratulation

you: tall, body taut as a violin string,
face glistening in the August evening,
insisting on reality

just this morning,
every morning, I woke
wearing the get-out-of-jail-free card
of my white skin

Night Court

Awake. Cold sweat beads your skin,
the red eye of the clock glares 2:15,
the comforter denies you comfort.

The room is quiet, but for the judge
and jury who assemble again tonight
to weigh your guilt, consider your crimes—
your sharp tongue, your loveless heart.

The prosecutor summons the witnesses, the lawyer
for the defense fails to appear. Dream evidence
is presented—that recurring young man frozen in a
toddler's body. What have you done to him?

Unforgiven, you thrash til dawn.
The judge calls a recess.
Case continued until tomorrow night.

Gender Studies

Any
boy
can
dream
extravagantly.
Fatefully,
girls
hope
in
judicious,
killjoy,
limiting
measure.
(Nicely.)
Only
paupered
quests
rest on
such
timid,
underfed
visions,
wordlessly
excising
youthful
zest.

Election 2016
    (after Wislawa Szymborska's Could Have)

Only a week after the unthinkable happened
it feels like it had to happen.
I didn't find out until later

that night, after the TV had been turned off.
I dreaded telling you—
you gave in to sleep first,

after knocking on doors even that last
day. And now, with the others,
we are left

in the shade
of a dark uncertainty, though that day broke sunny.
Strange fruit now ripens in my leafy, tree-

lined suburb. Swastikas sprout on immigrant churches. Break
glass in case of emergency. Surely this instant
qualifies. November 9th: that first night of broken glass from

Berlin to Vienna, when there was as little mercy or reprieve
as we may glimpse in coming days. Some wear safety pins through
their clothes to signify *I am safe* or

you can talk to me. This fragile gesture leaves me speechless.

How I Learned to Love the Hat
    On the Women's March, Jan. 21, 2017

No longer the object
of Trump's sneering assault,
no longer compliant,

they bobbed triumphant
on a million heads
like empresses borne aloft on their palanquins

hidden no longer
unspeakable no longer
no longer relegated to dark valleys and folds

(and did the Washington Monument
tremble just a bit, its
supremacy challenged?):

pussy.

On the Costa Brava

In Barceloneta, your grandmother would not be ashamed.
She would not protest gravity or curse her flesh.

Where did these Spanish women find their wisdom?
Not on the covers of *Vogue*, nor the runways of Milan,

but by the forgiving Mediterranean
where stretched and wrinkled bare breasts drop,
humbly, to receive the benediction of the sun.

III.

Life out of Order

She's a shocking flirt.
How she promises a tide
of picnics and puddings then like that
takes you on a furious funhouse ride
makes you eat ashes and dirt
a flood of ordure

then picks you up, smiles
and throws you a parade of roses.

Way Too Much and Not Enough

When the neighbor's son Ian
asks you for the phone, a match, a ride to the woods,
you remember him at

two; tasting cake for the first time, joyous, beneath your
oak trees, a dozen tiny lunatics colliding like billiard balls
on that sweet suburban August afternoon. Years later,

agitated accusations shrill from the house
nearby, crying and entreaties, slamming
doors, the swift and silent arrival of police cars.

Now he stands in your kitchen explaining to the
operator, *My dad is acting irrational, I'm not
the one who started it, I have a letter which says I'm sane.*

Even when you see him sitting on the curb
nowhere to go with his guitar and backpack
or shambling up your walk for the fifth time today, he is
undaunted, all he asks of you is a plastic bag in case it rains, a
glass of water, a ride to the entrance to the woods.

You leave him by the path with some roasted peppers and a slice of cake.

In Praise of Praise
    (In Memory of Mary Oliver 1935 – 2019)

It does not come easy.
The facile jab,
the heart-ripped cry "unfair"—
these are my natural tongue.

The world's pain,
the body's frailty,
the shortening clock
are my natural observation.

And yet the trembling dance of light-drunk
maple leaves, the honeyed rose petal,
clouds smudged with the last pink of the day,
the earthworm's blind progress
through winey spring loam—
all whisper of grace, of praise.

Unfinished

Who knew
when our sleep-famished eyes met
luminous
over the tops of their fragrant damp heads,
lovingly fingered infant comb-overs,
the scent of talc rising like yeast in new-made bread,
that years later,
free at last to finish our sentences
in cars and cafes
our empty laps would yearn
for the moist heaviness
of their quicksilver bodies,
our mouths still full of unsung lullabies
and kisses?

Flight Path

Today I practice the art of shelter-in-place,
collect batteries, flashlights, duct tape,

hoard water and toilet paper,
forswear adrenaline and instincts.

In my blood: expulsions, migrations,
the road, the sea, a nose for danger.

One step ahead
of the EgyptianSpanishRussian sheriff.

And would my ancestors have deigned
to join me

in the room away from the windows,
pass the chips and dip, await orders?

Or would they rise with a sigh,
hoist the samovars onto their backs,

the babies on their hips
and resume their flight?

Ode to Memory Loss

You've got some nerve telling me
that *thingy* is not a perfectly good word.
Better than good.
Hear how the first syllable resounds,
so solid, the adorable lilt at the end.

Vocabularies are too big these days.
Why, one's head could droop like the Elephant Man
just carrying all those words around.
So many of them superfluous
 or, as I like to say these days, too many.

And it's not just words.
Much has been made of Memory,
that la-dee-da lady with fancy clothes
and incessant stories. Proust and his infamous cookie,
his rows of memoirs on my shelf.

But I say I'm going to be a lot better off
when the shame
of slipping in someone's vomit
in seventh grade
leaves me.

They say one never forgets
how to ride a bicycle.
But I'd trade that one in a heartbeat
to remember the name of that apple-cheeked baby
whose picture sits on my dresser.

Poor Narcissus

So hard these days
getting pond-side
with your walker.

At the National Registry of Regret and Injustice

People wait for hours,
lines wrap around the building.

The claims are legion:
    wasn't allowed to go to the mall
couldn't have a baby
    studied all night and still flunked
 blind date was a jerk
    never met my parents
plane sat on the runway for three hours
    asshole cut me off in traffic
 couldn't love
    never learned to quilt.

Evening, applicants make for home,
stamped receipts between warm hands.

Larger cages, more desire

And who would call it crime
if the lady dares dream
of something racier
than the self-same meal,
accustomed, domestic.

No less than our four-legged friends,
we need to raid and roam
to quicken lust, escape the pallid cell.
For who can give a true embrace
                without egress?

Scenes from an April evening, 1933

The two girls have been sent out for the evening;
the boy, uncomprehending, can stay at home.
Best to keep him from the eyes of the neighbors—
his unfocused gaze and shuffling gait a *shanda*,
the family's disgrace.

Downstairs, folding
and unfolding The Jewish Advocate:
her husband of so many years,
still as eager as a boy for her.

Pregnant again.
Her mind and womb swelling with what-could-be.
Will the things that came automatically for other *kinder*
ever come at all for her son?

Two such children? No.

The doctor comes—and moves from bed to basin
with choreographed ease. As he works, voices drift
up from the street— men on stoops
argue politics in Yiddish.
Finally, that last rasping scrape.

In the street light's reflection,
the dirty instruments in the basin of soapy water glitter.
Dreamy from the pills the doctor gave her,
she imagines herself in a hospital,
a surgeon taking something from her belly—

a bullet, a diamond.

Additonal Acknowledgments

With gratitude towards my gentle first readers—Linda, Ellen, Mary Kay, and Shoshanna.

To Sandra Beasley, for her deft mentorship.

To Rachel, inveterate truth-teller, for her help with cover design and for a lifetime of laughter, delight, wonder and unwavering affection.

And to my constant supporter and cheerleader, Len, all my love.

Eileen Ivey Sirota is a psychotherapist, poet and potter. Her poems have appeared in *District Lines, Calyx, Beltway Poetry Quarterly, NewVerseNews* and elsewhere. In addition to practicing psychotherapy, Eileen is on the faculty at GWU School of Medicine, teaching prospective doctors to know their patients' stories as well as understand the mechanics of their bodies. Having been raised by a family of political junkies and activists in the Washington DC area, political and cultural issues infuse her poetry. She lives in Bethesda, Maryland.

www.ingramcontent.com/pod-product-compliance
Lightning Source LLC
LaVergne TN
LVHW041602070426
835507LV00011B/1270